WITHDRAWN

Your Body At Work

How Your Ears Work

by Carol Ballard

Gareth Stevens
Publishing

Please visit our Web site, www.garethstevens.com.
For a free color catalog of all our high-quality books,
call toll free 1-800-542-2595 or fax 1-877-542-2596.

Library of Congress Cataloging-in-Publication Data

Ballard, Carol.
How your ears work / Carol Ballard.
    p. cm. -- (Your body at work)
Includes index.
ISBN 978-1-4339-4106-1 (library binding)
1. Ear--Juvenile literature. 2. Hearing--Juvenile literature.
3. Ear--Diseases--Juvenile literature. I. Title.
QP462.2.B36 2011
612.8'5--dc22

                                        2010015859

This edition first published in 2011 by
Gareth Stevens Publishing
111 East 14th Street, Suite 349
New York, NY 10003

Editorial Director: Kerri O'Donnell
Design Director: Haley Harasymiw

Photo Credits:
Chapel Studios 5(top), 14, 16; Chris Fairclough Color Library 4, 23, 27; Robert Harding 6, 10;
Hearing Dogs For The Deaf 25; Cindy Minear/Shutterstock *cover*; Popperfoto 29; Teletec
International 24; Zefa 5(bottom), 22, contents page. The remaining pictures are from the
Wayland Picture Library.

Illustrations:
Kevin Jones Associates and Michael Courtney

Printed in China
CPSIA compliance information: Batch #WAS10GS: For further information contact Gareth Stevens, New York, New York at 1-800-542-2595.

Contents

Ears

Our ears are very important. We use them all the time to hear what is happening around us.

We use our ears to listen to the sounds of the natural world. It would be strange if we could not hear the birds singing.

We hear many different types of sound. Some give warnings, like fire and smoke alarms. Some sounds give information, like the announcements at airports and railroad stations, news bulletins, and weather reports. Alarm clocks wake us up and telephones ring to let us know someone wants to talk to us.

We listen to the radio and television for pleasure. Although television has pictures, you do need the sound, too. Try watching your favorite television show with the sound turned off and see what a difference it makes.

We use sound to communicate. We tell each other stories and jokes, and listen to each other's problems and secrets. This book will tell you more about your ears and how they work.

Our ears enable us to hear friends on the telephone. ▶

5

Parts of the Ear

Each ear has three sections: the outer ear, the middle ear, and the inner ear.

The outer ear consists of flaps on each side of your head called pinnae. They are made of cartilage, a stiff, bendy material that is covered with a layer of skin. Each pinna acts like a funnel, channeling sounds into the ear.

Elephants have enormous ear flaps to help keep them cool.

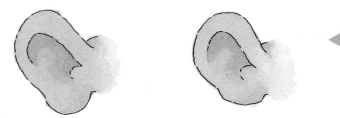

Look at your earlobes in a mirror. Are they curved or flat? Look at your family and friends' earlobes, too.

The bottom part of each pinna is called the lobe. It is softer than the rest of the pinna because it does not have any cartilage inside. Some people have curved earlobes while others have flat earlobes. The shape of your earlobe is passed down in families, in the same way as the color of your eyes and hair.

The rest of the outer ear is a tube called the auditory canal. Sounds travel along this tube to reach the middle ear.

skull bone

pinna

auditory canal

earlobe

The outer ear ▶

7

The Middle Ear

The middle ear is a tiny space filled with air. It is less than ¾ inch (20 mm) high and ⅕ inch (5 mm) wide. It is separated from the outer ear by the eardrum.

The eardrum is a thin sheet of skinlike material. It is stretched across the end of the auditory canal and is attached to a ring of bone.

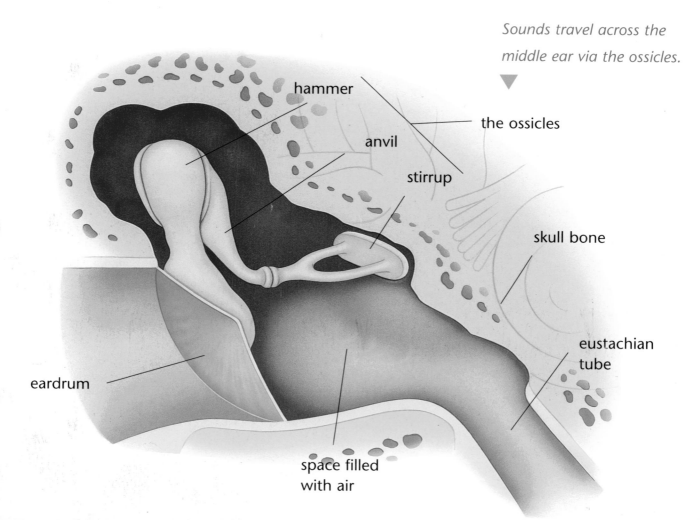

Sounds travel across the middle ear via the ossicles.

hammer

the ossicles

anvil

stirrup

skull bone

eustachian tube

eardrum

space filled with air

Inside the middle ear are the three smallest bones in the body: the hammer, anvil, and stirrup. Together, these are called the **ossicles**. They are linked together to form a chain of levers and are held in place by muscles and cords.

Your ears pop in an airplane because the air pressure changes, and the eustachian tube opens with a "pop" when you swallow.

The middle ear is linked to the space at the back of your nose by a tube. This tube is usually closed, but air can pass through it when it opens. This keeps the **air pressure** inside the middle ear the same as the pressure outside.

The thin eardrum is stretched tight like the skin on the top of a drum.

The Inner Ear

The inner ear is a complicated network of spaces and tubes, all filled with liquid.

The inner ear is separated from the middle ear by the oval window and the round window. These are very thin sheets of skinlike material stretched tightly across two gaps in the skull bone. They keep the liquid inside the inner ear and keep air out.

▲

The inner ear is sometimes called the labyrinth because it is like a maze of tubes. The labyrinth was a complicated maze. According to Greek legends, a monster named the Minotaur lived at the center of it.

◄ *The spiral cochlea is a little like a snail's shell. It gets its name from the Greek word for snail, kokhlos.*

The cochlea is a coiled, bony tube filled with liquid. It is lined with tiny hairs that play an important part in hearing. They are linked to the auditory nerve, which carries messages from your ear to your brain.

Also in your inner ear are three loops called semicircular canals. They are attached to a sac called the utriculus. These do not help you to hear, but they play an important part in keeping your body balanced.

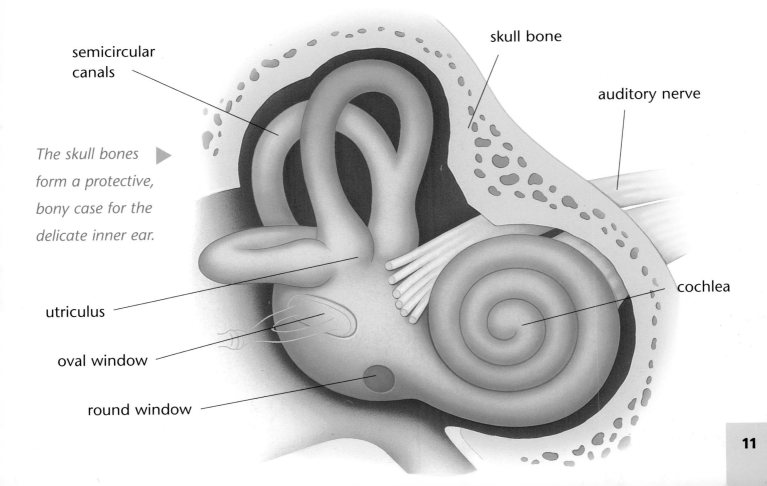

semicircular canals

skull bone

auditory nerve

The skull bones form a protective, bony case for the delicate inner ear.

utriculus

cochlea

oval window

round window

How Do Ears Work?

A sound is a very tiny movement in the air, called a wave. To hear a **sound wave**, it has to travel through your outer, middle, and inner ear.

1. Your pinnae channel sound waves into your ears.

2. The sound wave travels along the auditory canal.

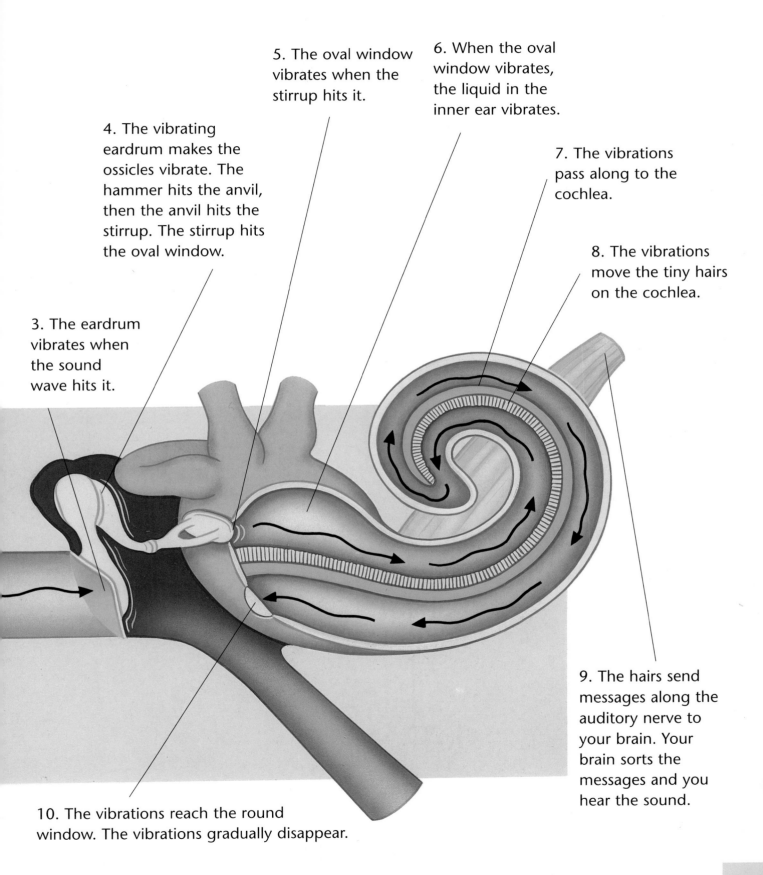

5. The oval window vibrates when the stirrup hits it.

6. When the oval window vibrates, the liquid in the inner ear vibrates.

4. The vibrating eardrum makes the ossicles vibrate. The hammer hits the anvil, then the anvil hits the stirrup. The stirrup hits the oval window.

7. The vibrations pass along to the cochlea.

8. The vibrations move the tiny hairs on the cochlea.

3. The eardrum vibrates when the sound wave hits it.

9. The hairs send messages along the auditory nerve to your brain. Your brain sorts the messages and you hear the sound.

10. The vibrations reach the round window. The vibrations gradually disappear.

Hearing Different Sounds

Think about some of the sounds you hear. Some, like birdsong, are high and others, like thunder, are low. How high or low a sound is we call its "pitch."

We can hear a wide range of pitch, but some sounds are too high or low for our ears to detect them. Some other animals can hear them—there are dog whistles that can be heard by dogs but not by humans.

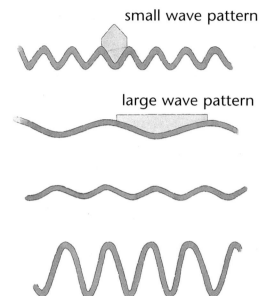

small wave pattern

large wave pattern

Different sounds have different wave patterns. Loud sounds have larger waves than quiet sounds.

◄ The thicker the string, the lower the sound it makes.

High-pitched sounds have waves very close together. Low-pitched sounds have waves farther apart. The inner end of the cochlea responds to the close wave patterns of high notes. The outer end of the cochlea responds to the spread out wave patterns of low notes.

Loud sounds have larger waves than quiet sounds, so they make larger vibrations inside your ear. Messages from your cochlea to your brain tell it how big the vibration was, so your brain can figure out how loud the sound is.

Do these instruments make high or low sounds? (A clue: the bigger the instrument, the lower the sounds it will make.)

Loud and Soft

The loudness of a sound is called its **intensity**. It is measured in **decibels**. We cannot hear a sound quieter than 0 decibels: this is the "threshold" of our hearing. Sounds can be quieter than 0 decibels, but our ears are not able to detect them.

Loud noises can damage our ears. People who use noisy equipment wear ear protectors to protect their ears. Loud music can damage our ears, too.

This woman wears ear protectors to protect her ears from the noise of the machinery.

Find out about the noises around you by conducting a sound survey. Choose your classroom, playground, and street. At each place, stand still for five minutes. Record the sounds you hear on a tape recorder or on paper. (You might need to decide on a code or shorthand so it does not take too long.) Look at your results to see which was the quietest place and which was the noisiest place.

decibels	
140	will damage ears
130	
120	
110	may damage ears
100	
90	
80	very loud
70	
60	
50	quiet
40	
30	
20	
10	very quiet
0	threshold of hearing

Record the sounds from your sound survey on a chart like this.

Balance

The three semicircular canals and utriculus in the inner ear help the body to stay still when we are sitting or standing, and to balance when we are moving around.

Travel sickness is caused by the brain receiving two different messages. The eyes tell the brain you are moving while the inner ears tell the brain you are still. To stop feeling sick, look ahead at the horizon so that your eyes will be still.

Inside each canal is a structure like a swing door. When you move your head, the liquid inside the canals pushes these doors open or shut. Tiny hairs inside the canals and utriculus detect this movement and send messages to your brain. The brain uses this information to figure out the new position of your head.

Have you ever spun around and around and then felt dizzy when you stopped? The liquid inside the utriculus cannot stop as quickly as your head. It keeps moving for a few seconds, so your brain still gets messages from it after you have stopped spinning.

Each canal lies in a different direction, up and down, right and left, and back and front. ▼

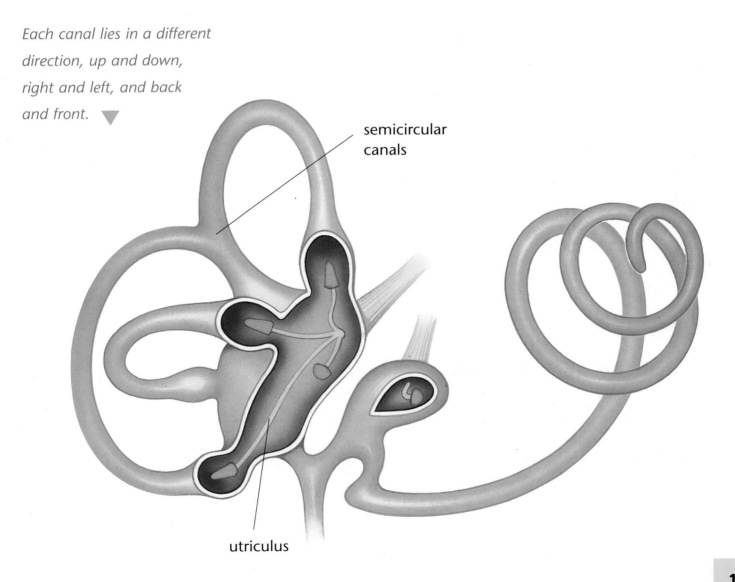

semicircular canals

utriculus

Using Two Ears

Have you ever
wondered why
you have two ears
and why there is
one on each side
of your head?

Some animals can move their
ears independently of each
other to help pinpoint exactly
where a sound is coming from.

Having two ears helps tell
the direction a sound has
come from. A sound will
reach one ear a fraction of a
second before it reaches the other.
It will also be a tiny amount louder
in one ear than in the other. The brain puts
together the information from both ears
and figures out where the sound came from.

Find the direction of a sound. Ask a friend to blindfold you and then to move a few steps away. Choose a noise, like clapping hands. Ask your friend to make this noise from different positions. Can you tell exactly where your friend is? Now repeat the test first with your left ear covered and then with your right ear covered. Can you still tell where your friend is?

These children are trying to find out whether two ears are better than one.

How Well Can You Hear?

Not being able to hear properly can cause problems with learning. Doctors and nurses test how well babies and young children can hear, but unless the problems are serious, they are often not noticed until a child starts school.

▲

Ear trumpets were used before modern hearing aids were invented. They acted as enormous pinnae, channeling more sound waves into the ear.

◀ *A doctor may use a special audiometer to test a baby's hearing.*

A hearing specialist will check whether the child can hear high and low sounds, and loud and quiet sounds. Then the specialist will try to find out why the child cannot hear properly. He or she will check to see whether the outer ear is blocked, and may also examine the eardrum using a special instrument called an otoscope. An otoscope also allows the middle ear to be seen. Any signs of infection or other problems can be detected.

Many people, as they get older, suffer gradual loss of hearing. They may decide to have a hearing aid fitted.

These girls are deaf so they use hearing aids and sign language.

Deafness

Deaf people need special help so that they can lead independent lives. Machines are designed to help deaf people do everyday activities. They may use a telephone with a printer to write what the caller says. A light may flash when somebody presses the doorbell. Deaf people may use hearing aids. These are tiny microphones that fit inside their ear and make sounds louder.

◀ The screen on this telephone lets a deaf person see what the caller is saying.

Some deaf people have "hearing dogs." These dogs are trained to alert their deaf owners to sounds such as the doorbell, telephone, and alarm clock. Instead of barking, the dog is taught to touch its owner and then lead them to the sound.

Many deaf people can understand what other people are saying by lipreading. They watch carefully as the person talks, and figure out what is being said from the shapes and movements of their lips.

A hearing dog can help a deaf person to do things we take for granted. ▶

Sign Language

Many deaf people use **sign language** to help them to communicate with other people.

Sign language has been used for hundreds of years. In medieval monasteries, monks in "silent orders" were not allowed to speak, so they used sign language to communicate with each other. There are still some monasteries like this today.

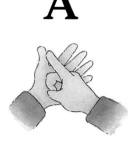

A

B

C

D

Here, the first four letters of the finger alphabet can be seen. ▶

◀ *These children are using sign language.*

There are two types of sign, those for whole words and those for single letters. Words that are used a lot have their own sign. These are often **gestures** that we use naturally, like a shiver to say "cold," "thumbs up" to say "OK," and shrugging shoulders to say "I don't know."

Words that are not used often do not have their own signs. Instead, they have to be spelled out one letter at a time, using an "alphabet" of finger and hand positions.

Children who are born deaf often find it difficult to learn to talk. Their teacher uses sign language instead of talking to them.
▼

Look After Your Ears

It is important to look after your ears. Here are some suggestions about how to keep your ears healthy.

Try to keep them clean and free from too much wax. Never stick anything inside your ear, it could get stuck.

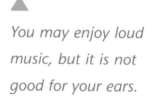

You may enjoy loud music, but it is not good for your ears.

Loud noises can damage your ears, so try to avoid them if you can. When listening to your MP3 player, make sure the volume is not too high. Try not to use earphones for long spells without a break. Avoid spending too much time in very noisy places.

If you take part in an activity where ear protection is provided, then make sure you use it.

If you have had problems with your ears, follow the advice of your doctor. You may have to stop activities such as swimming for a while, but it is only for a short time and your ears have to last you a lifetime.

It can be noisier at a rock concert than in some factories. ▶

Glossary

air pressure The force of air pushing against something.

decibel The measure of how loud a sound is.

gestures Movements of the hands, head, or body to show feelings.

hearing aid A device that helps people with hearing loss to hear better.

inner ear A complicated network of spaces and tubes filled with liquid.

intensity The loudness of a sound.

maze Paths and passages designed to puzzle those walking through them.

middle ear A tiny space that houses the ossicles.

ossicles The three tiny bones in the middle ear—the hammer, anvil, and stirrup.

pitch How high or low a sound is.

sign language A system of gestures used by deaf people instead of speech.

sound wave The movement of sound through air.

vibrate To move backward and forward very quickly.

Further Reading

Books to Read

Body Focus: Ears
by Carol Ballard
Heinemann-Raintree, 2009

The Sense of Hearing
by Elaine Landau
Children's Press, 2009

Web Sites

http://kidshealth.org/kid/htbw/ears.html

http://library.thinkquest.org/3750/hear/hear.html

Index

Donated to

SAINT PAUL PUBLIC LIBRARY

ANNA GROSSNICKLE HINES

WHEN THE GOBLINS CAME KNOCKING

 GREENWILLOW BOOKS, NEW YORK

The full-color art was prepared with colored
pencils on black paper.
The text type is Plantin.
Printed in Hong Kong
by South China Printing Company (1988) Ltd.
First Edition
10 9 8 7 6 5 4 3 2 1

Library of Congress
Cataloging-in-Publication Data

Hines, Anna Grossnickle.
When the goblins came knocking /
by Anna Grossnickle Hines.
p. cm.
Summary: Last Halloween was
a scary experience because of walking
pumpkins, haunting ghosts, flying
witches, and other disturbing sights,
but this Halloween will be different.
ISBN 0-688-13735-0 (trade).
ISBN 0-688-13736-9 (lib. bdg.)
[1. Halloween—Fiction.
2. Stories in rhyme.]
I. Title.   PZ8.3.H556Wh
1995   [E]—dc20
94-19366   CIP   AC

FOR JOCELYN AND ROY,
WHO HELP CHILDREN
AND THOSE WHO WORK WITH CHILDREN
UNDERSTAND THEIR FEELINGS

When the pumpkins came walking,
creeping and peeking,
sneakily stalking,
last Halloween . . .

I was tongue-tied.

When the ghosties came haunting,
moaning and groaning,
booing and taunting,
last Halloween . . .

I wanted to hide.

When the witches came flying,
screeching and cackling,
swooping and crying,
last Halloween . . .
I ran, terrified.

When the ghoulies came prancing,
smirking and grinning,
leaping and dancing,
last Halloween . . .
I trembled inside.

When the monsters came yowling,
screaming and shrieking,
yelling and howling,
last Halloween . . .
I whined and I cried.

When the goblins came knocking,
tricking and treating,
spooking and mocking,
last Halloween . . .
I was too scared to join in the fun.

But *this* Halloween